Potato Chip Cookies
&
Tomato Soup Cake:
Recipes of Americana

Edited by Carole Eberly
Illustrations by Kathi Terry

eberly press
403 Frankfort Ave.
P.O. Box 305
Elberta, MI 49628

Copyright 1992 - Carole Eberly

Printed in USA

ISBN 0-932296-15-7

About this book...

While surveying my cookbook collection, I noticed something peculiar—the down-home, bizarre and fun books were falling apart or the pages were glued together by egg whites, milk or "stuff." The ones written by Chief Pierre of "Le Too Expensive For You" restaurant were as pristine as the day I bought them. Whether at a local garage sale or at a second-hand store in New Orleans, San Antonio or Boston, I always look for the slightly strange cookbooks—the ones containing recipes you would have a tough time explaining to someone from a friendly planet.

But what really got me thinking was the day Keith Greenwood showed up at an office potluck with his Aunt Connie's Dirt Cake. Since this concoction was in a flower pot (complete with plastic flower), everyone thought it was a centerpiece. It really looked like dirt in there. We all finished eating, when we noticed a chagrined look on Keith's face. "Isn't anyone going to eat this," he asked an astonished audience. "Eat dirt? Eat dirt, yourself," was the collective thought. But, after some coaxing, we did eat dirt—and it was great! He kept the copy machine hot for the next three hours running off copies of Dirt Cake for everyone.

So, here you will find some favorite oddball recipes shared by family and friends on old napkins, matchbook covers and recipe cards adorned with hearts and flowers. They have names and ingredients only Americans could dream up.

Hold the escargot; bring on the Wacky Cake.

Carole Eberly

Contents

Appetizers

&

Snacks

Nuts & Bolts

(Great for winter nights in front of the TV or summer nights at the cottage in front of the jigsaw puzzle)

  2 cups Rice Chex
  2 cups Wheat Chex
  2 cups Corn Chex
  4 ounces small round pretzels
  1 cup salted peanuts
  1 stick butter
  2 tablespoons Worcestershire sauce
  ½ teaspoon garlic powder

Mix cereal, pretzels and peanuts together in a large roasting pan. Melt butter; stir in Worcestershire and garlic powder. Pour over cereal mixture, coating as evenly as possible. Cover and bake at 225 degrees for 1 hour, stirring occasionally.

Spinach Dip

1 package frozen spinach
1 cup sour cream
1 box dry Knorr's vegetable soup
1 cup chopped water chestnuts
1 cup mayonnaise
1 round loaf dark pumpernickel bread

Defrost spinach and squeeze out the water. Stir spinach into remaining ingredients. Cut off bread--about 2-inch slice. Scoop out bread and cut, along with top, into 2-inch cubes. Fill bread shell with spinach dip. Use cubes for dipping.

Mock Boursin Cheese

(Why pay more? Make your own.)

1 8-ounce package cream cheese
¼ cup butter (not margarine)
1 clove minced garlic
¼ teaspoon salt
⅛ teaspoon thyme
⅛ teaspoon basil
⅛ teaspoon marjoram
⅛ teaspoon dill weed
⅛ teaspoon pepper
⅛ teaspoon parsley
¼ teaspoon red wine vinegar

Beat cream cheese and butter until thoroughly blended. Add remaining ingredients, mixing well. Pack in a container and chill several hours. Serve at room temperature with crackers.

Turtle Sundaes

2 teaspoons butter
¼ cup pecan halves
½ cup caramel sauce
½ cup chocolate sauce
4 large scoops vanilla ice cream

Melt butter in a small saucepan. Add pecans and cook over medium-low heat, stirring occasionally, for 4-5 minutes or until pecans begin to brown. In a glass measuring cup, pour in caramel and chocolate sauces. Stir only once. Warm slightly in microwave oven. Scoop ice cream into serving dishes. Divide sauce among the dishes. Top with pecans.

Chocolate Waffles

(Put a scoop of ice cream and chocolate sauce on top for desert)

2 cups flour
3 teaspoons baking powder
½ teaspoon salt
3 tablespoons cocoa
¼ cup sugar
2 eggs, separated
¼ cup melted butter
1¼ cups milk
½ teaspoon vanilla

Sift flour, baking power, salt, cocoa and sugar together into a mixing bowl. Beat egg yolks, butter, milk and vanilla. Stir into flour mixture. Beat eggs whites until stiff; fold into waffle mixture. Fill hot, greased waffle iron with batter and bake until browned.

Marshmallow Hats

(Kids' time in the kitchen!)

1 12-ounce package chocolate chips
1 tablespoon salad oil
1 small package shredded coconut
30 large marshmallows

Melt chocolate with oil in top of double boiler. Pour coconut into a shallow dish. Dip each marshmallow into chocolate, then coat with coconut. Place flat side down on cookie sheet lined with waxed paper. Chill until chocolate is set—about 10 minutes.

Puppy Chow

½ cup semi-sweet chocolate chips
½ cup butterscotch chips
½ cup chunky peanut butter
½ cup butter
1 box Rice or Corn Chex
1 cup powdered sugar

Melt chips, peanut butter and butter in saucepan. Pour cereal in large bowl; cover with chip mixture. Stir until cereal is coated. Pour powdered sugar in large container with lid; add the cereal. Cover with lid and shake until cereal is covered with sugar.

7-Layer Taco Dip

1 small can jalapeño bean dip
2 ripe avocados
1 tablespoon lemon juice
3 tablespoons mayonnaise
2 tablespoons sour cream
½ package taco seasoning
¼ cup shredded cheddar cheese
¼ cup shredded Monterey Jack cheese
2 chopped and seeded tomatoes
8 chopped green onions
1 cup sliced black olives

Spread bean dip in bottom of a glass pie plate. In small bowl, mash avocados with lemon juice. Spread over bean dip. In small bowl, mix mayonnaise, sour cream and taco seasoning. Spread on top of avocados. Sprinkle with cheddar and Monterey cheese. Sprinkle with tomatoes, onions and black olives.

April Fool's Ice Cream Cones

1 large box cake mix
20-24 flat bottom ice cream cones
1 can prepared frosting

Mix up the cake batter. Fill cones ⅔ full. Bake standing up on a cookie sheet at 350 degrees for 25 minutes. Cool. Frost.

Party Dogs

Bourbon
Catsup
Brown sugar
Hot dogs

In a large saucepan, mix equal parts of bourbon, brown sugar and catsup. Simmer 20 minutes over low heat. Chop hot dogs into 5 pieces and add to mixture, being careful to allow mixture to cover. Simmer uncovered for 40 minutes. Serve in chafing dish with toothpicks.

Biddy on a Bun

2 cups chopped cooked chicken
1 cup minced celery
2 tablespoons relish
½ teaspoon seasoned salt
¼ teaspoon pepper
⅔ cup mayonnaise
6 hamburger buns
6 ounces shredded cheddar cheese
12 stuffed olives

Mix together chicken, celery, relish, salt, pepper and mayonnaise. Split buns and toast under broiler. Spread chicken mixture on buns. Top each with cheese. Broil 2 minutes or until cheese is melted. Top each with an olive.

Wing Dings

3 pounds chicken wings, tips removed
½ cup sugar
⅓ cup vinegar
½ cup catsup
2 tablespoons flour
1 teaspoon salt
½ teaspoon onion powder
½ teaspoon dry mustard
¼ teaspoon ground cloves
⅛ teaspoon minced garlic

Place chicken in a shallow baking pan. In a saucepan, mix remaining ingredients. Bring to a boil, stirring constantly. Lower heat to simmer and cook, while stirring, for 2 minutes. Pour sauce over chicken. Cover and bake at 350 degrees for 30 minutes. Remove cover and bake for another 30 minutes. Serve cold or hot.

Peanut Butter & Bacon Hors d'oeuvres

Ritz crackers
Peanut butter
Bacon

Spread peanut butter on crackers. Fry bacon until crisp. Crumble on top of peanut butter. Voila.

Baloney Bean Boats

(It's time to return to elementary school days)

Baloney
Baked beans

Fry baloney in skillet until the edges curl up to form a "boat." Fill with heated baked beans.

Potato Skins

2 medium potatoes
Butter
2 tablespoons melted butter
¼ cup grated cheddar cheese
¼ cup crumbled crispy bacon

Rub potatoes with butter to keep skin soft. Bake at 375 degrees for 1 hour. Remove from oven. Cut lengthwise into quarters. Scoop out potato, leaving ¼ inch next to skin. Brush potatoes with melted butter. Sprinkle with cheese and bacon. Bake at 375 degrees for 20 minutes.

Cheese Straws

1½ cup grated extra sharp cheddar cheese
1 stick butter
1½ cups flour
¼ teaspoon salt
¼ teaspoon paprika
4 tablespoons ice water

Cream cheese and butter. Add remaining ingredients. Mix well. Roll out thin—about ⅛-inch thick—on lightly floured board. Cut in strips about ½-inch wide. Place on ungreased baking sheet. Bake at 350 degrees for 15 minutes. Makes about 30.

Beverages

Slush

(Serves lots of people on a hot summer day)

>   9 cups water
>   2 cups sugar
>   1 12-ounce can orange juice concentrate
>   1 12-ounce can lemonade concentrate
>   2½ cups vodka

Heat water and sugar together until sugar dissolves. Remove from heat and stir in remaining ingredients. Pour into large bowl or plastic container. Freeze. Scoop out about ½ cup of mixture per serving into a glass. Fill with ginger ale or 7-Up.

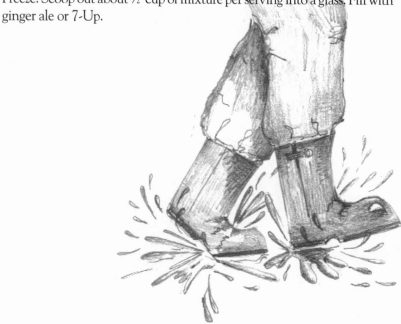

Percolator Punch

3 cups pineapple juice
2 cups cranberry juice
½ cup water
⅓ cup brown sugar
1 teaspoon whole cloves
1 teaspoon whole allspice
3 sticks cinnamon

Pour juices and water in bottom of percolator. Put sugar and spices in basket of percolator. Perk. Serve hot.

Hot Chocolate Mix

(Add 1 cup miniature marshmallows to the mix if you want—you can also substitute 1 cup dry coffee creamer for 1 cup of powdered milk for a richer drink)

4 cups powdered milk
¾ cup cocoa
1 ½ cups sugar
½ teaspoon cinnamon (optional)
⅛ teaspoon salt

Put into a container and shake until well mixed. To make, put 3 tablespoons mixture in small amount of boiling water, stirring to make a paste. When milk is dissolved, fill cup with hot water.

Irish Cream

2 cups half & half
2 cups whiskey
1 14-ounce can sweetened condensed milk
1 teaspoon instant coffee granules
¼ cup coffee liqueur

Mix ingredients together and pour into jar with lid. Keep refrigerated. Stir once a day for 1 week.

Cherry Bounce

2 quarts tart cherries (no need to pit)
2 pounds sugar
2 fifths whiskey

Mix all ingredients together in
large jar with a lid. Cover. Stir
once a day for the first week;
weekly thereafter. Strain and
bottle anytime after 2 months.

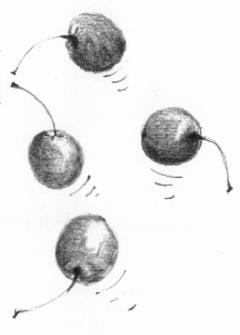

Coffee Liqueur

1 quart vodka
4 cups sugar
6 tablespoons freeze dried coffee
1 split vanilla bean
1⅓ cups water

Mix ingredients together and pour in large jar with lid. Stir twice a day for 2 weeks.

Hot Buttered Rum

½ cup butter
2 cups brown sugar
¼ teaspoon cinnamon
¼ teaspoon nutmeg
¼ teaspoon cloves
Dark rum
Boiling water

Cream butter and sugar. Add spices, beating until well mixed. Transfer into covered container and store in refrigerator up to 2 months. To use, place 1 tablespoon of mix in bottom of mug. Add 1½ ounces dark rum. Fill mug with boiling water.

Sun Tea

(Grab your love beads)

10 tea bags
Water
Sun

Remove paper tags from tea bags. Place bags in bottom of 1 gallon jar. Fill with cold water. Set in sun for 6-7 hours or until tea is strength you like. Remove tea bags and refrigerate jar.

Orange Drink ...like at the mall!!

1 6-ounce can orange juice
1 cup milk
1 cup water
½ cup sugar
1 teaspoon vanilla
12 ice cubes

Throw all ingredients in blender and blast. Makes 4-6 servings.

Russian Tea

(Remember giving this as a Christmas gift?)

½ cup Tang
⅓ cup instant tea
¼ cup sugar
¼ teaspoon cinnamon
⅛ teaspoon cloves
3 tablespoons powdered lemonade mix

Mix all ingredients well. Use 1 tablespoon per cup of boiling water.

Salads,

Vegetables

&

Jellies

Sauerkraut Salad

(A good one for summer get-togethers)

> 1 1-pound, 11-ounce can sauerkraut
> 1 cup diced green pepper
> 1 cup diced celery
> ¼ cup diced onion
> ¼ cup vinegar
> ½ cup salad oil
> ½ cup sugar
> 2 tablespoons diced pimentos

Drain sauerkraut well. Mix all ingredients together in a large bowl. Cover and chill overnight. Serves 8-10.

Copper Pennies

> 2 pounds carrots
> 1 green pepper
> 1 medium onion
> 1 can tomato soup
> ½ cup salad oil
> 1 cup sugar
> ¾ cup vinegar
> 1 teaspoon mustard
> 1 teaspoon Worcestershire sauce
> Salt
> Pepper

Slice carrots into rounds and cook until tender. Slice pepper and onion. Place in bowl with carrots. Mix remaining ingredients in a bowl. Pour over vegetables and chill several hours, stirring occasionally.

Five Cup Salad

1 cup mandarin orange sections
1 cup pineapple chunks
1 cup whipped topping
1 cup miniature marshmallows
1 cup coconut

Mix all ingredients together and chill.

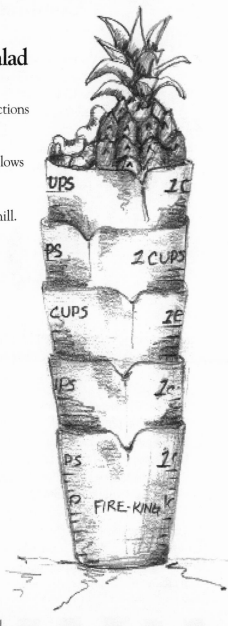

Coca-Cola Salad

1 small box orange gelatin
1 3-ounce package cream cheese
1¼ cups Coca-Cola
½ cup chopped walnuts

Stir gelatin into softened cream cheese. Heat cola to boiling and pour over gelatin mixture. Stir in nuts and pour into mold. Let stand 1 hour before chilling. Salad will separate into three layers.

Spaghetti Fruit Salad

2 eggs
1 can pineapple chunks
¼ cup pineapple juice
1 cup powdered sugar
3 peeled and cubed apples
1 cup cooked and drained spaghetti
1 cup whipped topping

Beat eggs. Drain pineapple chunks; saving juice. Pour ¼ cup of juice in with eggs and beat well. Beat in sugar. Cook over low heat until thick. Cool; add fruit and spaghetti. Chill thoroughly, about 8 hours. Before serving, stir in whip cream.

Frozen Fruit Salad

1 8-ounce package cream cheese
1 cup mayonnaise
2 cans drained fruit cocktail
2 cups miniature marshmallows
1 cup whipping cream
2 tablespoons powdered sugar

Beat cream cheese and mayonnaise until blended. Stir in fruit cocktail. Fold in marshmallows. Beat whipping cream until soft peaks form. Beat in powdered sugar. Fold into fruit cocktail mixture. Pour into 8-inch square pan. Wrap and freeze about 3 hours.

8-Layer Salad

(Required at any potluck in the '70s)

4 cups chopped lettuce
1 cup chopped celery
1 cup sliced water chestnuts
1 cup chopped onion
1 cup frozen peas
1 cup shredded cheddar cheese
¼ cup fried and crumbled bacon
1½ cups mayonnaise

Put each ingredient into large bowl in order given. Chill several hours or overnight.

Heavenly Hash

½ pound marshmallows
1 large can crushed pineapple (drained)
½ cup chopped walnuts
2 cups whipped topping

Cut marshmallows in quarters with scissors. Fold all ingredients together. Chill.

Pretzel Salad

2 cups crushed pretzels
½ cup sugar
¾ cup butter
1 8-ounce package cream cheese
½ cup sugar
1 small carton whipped topping
1 large box strawberry flavored gelatin
2 cups boiling water
2 10-ounce packages frozen strawberries

Mix pretzels, sugar and butter together. Spread in 9x13-inch pan and bake at 350 degrees for 10 minutes. Cool. Beat cream cheese, sugar and topping together. Spread on pretzel mixture. Dissolve gelatin in boiling water. Stir in strawberries. Chill until partially set. Spread on top of cream cheese mixture and chill.

Pistachio Pudding Salad

1 small box pistachio pudding mix
1 large can undrained crushed pineapple
1 cup miniature marshmallows
½ cup chopped walnuts or pecans
1 small carton whipped topping

In a serving bowl, stir pudding into the pineapple until mixed. Stir in marshmallows and nuts. Fold in whipped topping. Chill.

Make-Ahead Mashed Potatoes

(At last—a recipe that let's you worry about getting the other things together at Thanksgiving. This is one of our favorites —we cheerfully eat the leftovers for days.)

8 large peeled, cooked and drained potatoes
1 8-ounce package cream cheese
½ cup sour cream
2 teaspoons salt
¼ teaspoon pepper
Butter
Paprika

Mash potatoes until lumps are gone. Beat in cream cheese, sour cream, salt and pepper. When light and fluffy, put into greased 9x13-inch baking dish. Cover with tin foil and refrigerate up to one week. Before serving, dot with butter, sprinkle with paprika and bake at 350 for 30 minutes.

Painted Cabbage

4 strips bacon
1 small head shredded red cabbage
Water
1 tablespoon sugar
¼ cup vinegar

Fry bacon in non-stick pan until crisp; crumble. Add cabbage with a small amount of water. Cover and simmer 10 minutes. Add sugar and vinegar; cook uncovered 5 minutes.

STOP!

(A favorite of backyard gardeners)

> 5 small yellow squash
> 2 tomatoes
> 1 large onion
> 1½ large green peppers
> 1 stick butter
> Salt & pepper

Slice vegetables. In a baking dish, create 2-3 layers of squash, pepper, onion and tomatoes. Dot each layer with butter. Sprinkle with salt and pepper. Bake at 350 degrees for 1 hour. Serves 4-6.

Tomato Pudding

2 slices white bread
½ cup melted butter
1 10 ½-ounce can tomato puree
⅔ cup brown sugar

Cut bread into 1-inch cubes. Place in 8-inch square baking dish. Pour melted butter over bread cubes. In a small saucepan, bring tomato puree and brown sugar to a boil. Pour over the buttered bread. Prick bread cubes until saturated with tomato mixture. Bake uncovered at 400 degrees for 20-25 minutes.

Carrot Marmalade

2 pounds raw, grated carrots
2 lemons
1 orange
1 cup seedless golden raisins
1 cup sugar for each cup of mixture
Dash of cinnamon & nutmeg

Place carrots in a large kettle. Seed lemons and orange; slice (leave peel on) very thin. Add to kettle. Add raisins and sugar. Stir in spices. Boil gently for 30 minutes, stirring often to prevent sticking. Pour into sterile jars and seal with melted wax. Store in refrigerator.

Corncob Jelly

12 corncobs
6 cups water
1 package powdered fruit pectin
3 cups sugar

Boil corncobs in water 30 minutes. Remove and strain, saving the juice. Add enough water to make 3 cups and pour into pan. Stir in fruit pectin and bring to a boil. Add sugar and boil 2-3 minutes, stirring constantly. Pour into jelly glasses. Cool and seal. Makes about 3 cups.

Pepper Jelly

(Great with crackers and cream cheese)

> 6 large green peppers
> 1½ cups vinegar
> 1 teaspoon hot pepper sauce
> 1 6-ounce bottle Certo
> 6½ cups sugar
> Green food coloring

Seed peppers. Process in three batches with vinegar and hot pepper sauce in blender. Pour into large kettle. Add Certo and bring to rolling boil. Add sugar and boil 1 minute. Remove from heat. Add a few drops food coloring. Stir and skim. Pour into sterile jars and seal.

Cucumber Jelly

> 3-4 cucumbers
> 1 cup vinegar
> ½ cup water
> 7 cups white sugar
> 1 6-ounce bottle Certo
> Few drops of green food coloring

Peel and seed cucumbers. Liquefy in blender. Measure 2 cups of liquid. Pour into a large pot with vinegar, water and sugar. Boil for 2 minutes on high heat, stirring constantly. Remove from heat. Add Certo and food coloring. Pour jelly into jars. Cool before putting on lids. Makes about 4-5 cups. Good with meats and poultry.

Carrot Syrup

1 large grated carrot
Juice and rind of 1 lemon
2 cups sugar
2 cups water
¼ teaspoon powered ginger

Mix all ingredients in medium saucepan. Simmer until syrup thick-
ens. Strain.

Dandelion Jelly

(Well, here's something to do with your lawn this summer)

    1 quart dandelion blossoms
    1 quart water
    1 package powdered fruit pectin
    2 tablespoons lemon juice
    5 cups sugar
    4 drops yellow food coloring

Rinse blossoms well; place in saucepan with water and bring to a boil. Simmer 5 minutes. Strain out 3 cups of dandelion juice, pressing blossoms with fingers. Return to saucepan with lemon juice and pectin. Bring to a boil and add sugar, stirring constantly. Bring to a boil again and boil 3 minutes. Stir in food coloring. Pour into sterile jars and seal.

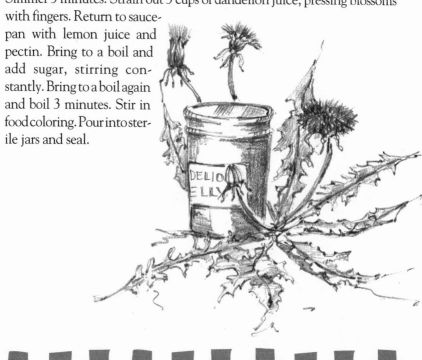

Beet Jelly

3 cups beet juice
1 package powdered fruit pectin
1 package powdered grape drink mix
4 cups sugar

Combine beet juice, drink mix and pectin in a saucepan. Bring to a full boil, stirring constantly. Stir in sugar and boil again. Cook 1 minute. Pour into sterile glasses and seal.

Main Dishes

Spaghetti Pie

1½ pounds ground beef or turkey
1 medium chopped onion
1 stalk chopped celery
½ teaspoon minced garlic
1 16-ounce can tomatoes
1 6-ounce can tomato paste
1 teaspoon basil
¼ teaspoon salt
⅛ teaspoon pepper
6 ounces spaghetti
¼ cup melted butter
⅓ cup grated Parmesan cheese
2 beaten eggs
1 cup cottage cheese
1½ cups shredded mozzarella cheese

Brown meat and drain. Add onion, celery and garlic; saute until tender. Stir in tomatoes, tomato paste and seasonings. Cover and simmer 20 minutes. Cook spaghetti; drain. Mix in butter, Parmesan cheese and eggs. Line a greased 10-inch pie plate with spaghetti to form a crust. Spoon cottage cheese over crust. Top with meat sauce and mozzarella cheese. Bake at 325 degrees for 45 minutes. Serves 6-8.

Pizza-Stuffed Peppers

¼ pound ground beef
¼ cup diced onion
½ cup grated mozzarella cheese
½ cup pizza sauce
¼ teaspoon Italian seasoning
2 medium green peppers

Brown meat and onion. Add remaining ingredients, except peppers. Cook and stir until cheese is slightly melted. Halve and seed peppers. Arrange peppers in baking dish; spoon mixture into peppers. (Sprinkle with a little more cheese, if desired.) Bake at 350 degrees for 15-20 minutes.

Johnny Marzetti

(Straight out of 1950 school cafeterias. Who was Johnny Marzetti, anyway?)

1 pound ground beef
1 medium chopped onion
1 1-pound can tomatoes
1 teaspoon salt
⅛ teaspoon garlic salt
⅛ teaspoon pepper
½ pound grated cheese (whatever is on hand)
1 6-ounce package wide noodles

Brown meat and onions in non-stick skillet. Stir in remaining ingredients, except noodles, saving out ½ cup cheese. Cook noodles; drain and add to meat mixture. Cover and simmer for 20 minutes. Sprinkle with remaining cheese before serving.

City Chicken

(During my college days, we were served city chicken about once a week in the dorm. For four years we tried to figure out what city chicken really was or how it got that name—no one found out. However, this recipe provides the answer to one of our questions.)

½ pound veal, cut into 1-inch cubes
½ pound lean pork, cut into 1-inch cubes
½ pound beef steak, cut into 1-inch cubes
1½ cups fine dry bread crumbs
1 teaspoon seasoned salt
¼ teaspoon pepper
1 egg
1 tablespoon water
¼ cup shortening
½ cup water

Alternate veal, pork and beef cubes on 5-inch wooden skewers. Mix bread crumbs, salt and pepper together on a plate. Beat egg with water in a pie pan. Roll skewered meat into bread crumbs, dip in egg and roll in bread crumbs again. Heat shortening in frying pan. Brown meat on all sides. Pour in water and cover tightly. Simmer for 45 minutes or until meat is tender. Serves 4-6. (Multiply by 500 for a dorm complex—more if football players live there.)

Five Can Casserole

(For SIX CAN CASSEROLE, add 1 4-ounce can sliced water chestnuts)

1 small can boned chicken
1 small can evaporated milk
1 can cream of chicken soup
1 can cream of mushroom soup
1 5-ounce can chow mein noodles

Stir all ingredients together in a bowl. Pour into greased 8-inch square dish and bake at 350 degrees for 25 minutes.

Impossible Ham & Cheese Pie

2 cups diced ham
1 cup shredded Swiss cheese
¼ cup chopped onion
4 eggs
2 cups milk
1 cup Bisquick
Salt
Pepper

In the bottom of a greased 10-inch pie plate, sprinkle ham, cheese and onions. Beat remaining ingredients. Pour over ham mixture. Bake at 400 degrees until golden brown, about 35-40 minutes.

Paper Bag Chicken

Shortening
1 cut up chicken
1 cup barbecue sauce

Grease inside of paper bag with shortening; place inside of another paper bag—greased side will touch chicken. Wash and dry chicken. Brush pieces with barbecue sauce until well-coated. Place chicken in paper bag; tie a wire twist or string. Bake on a cookie sheet at 325 degrees for 2 hours or until done.

Shipwreck

(Flashback to Girl Scout days)

>3 large sliced potatoes
>2 large chopped onions
>1½ pounds ground beef
>2 celery stalks
>½ cup uncooked rice
>1 can kidney beans
>2 cans tomato soup
>Salt
>Pepper

Put potatoes, onions, beef, celery, rice and kidney beans in a greased baking dish. Season with salt and pepper. Pour soup over the top. Cover and bake at 350 degrees for about 2 hours (or until it burns over a campfire).

Cornflake Chicken

>4 cups cornflakes
>1 teaspoon salt
>1 teaspoon parsley flakes
>¼ teaspoon pepper
>1 egg
>2 tablespoons milk
>1 cut-up chicken or 4 chicken breasts

Finely crush cornflakes. Pour into a small paper bag. Pour in salt, parsley and pepper; shake until well mixed. Beat egg and milk in pie plate. Dip chicken in egg mixture. Shake in paper bag until coated. Place chicken pieces in baking pan and bake at 400 degrees for 1 hour.

Cola Roast

1 teaspoon salt
½ teaspoon pepper
½ teaspoon garlic powder
1 4-5 pound roast
3 tablespoons salad oil
1½ cups cola
12 ounces chili sauce
3 tablespoons Worcestershire sauce
2 tablespoons hot sauce

Mix salt, pepper and garlic powder together; rub over roast. Brown roast in oil; drain. Combine remaining ingredients and pour over roast in covered baking pan. Cover and bake at 325 degrees for 3 hours, or until tender.

Porcupines

1 pound ground beef
½ cup chopped onion
½ cup uncooked rice
½ cup water
1 teaspoon celery salt
⅛ teaspoon pepper
⅛ teaspoon garlic powder
1 15-ounce can tomato sauce
1 cup water
3 tablespoons Worcestershire sauce
1 teaspoon sugar

Mix ground beef, onion, rice, ½ cup water, celery salt, pepper, and garlic powder in a bowl. Shape into tablespoon-sized balls. Brown meatballs in about 2 tablespoons of shortening in a frying pan. Drain. Stir in remaining ingredients. Cover and simmer about 45 minutes, adding more water if needed

Potato Chip Finger Chicken

1 pound boneless chicken breasts
1 can Pringle's potato chips
½ cup melted butter

Cut chicken into 2-inch strips. Put about ¾ can of Pringle's into a plastic bag and crush with rolling pin. Dip chicken into melted butter; shake a few at a time in plastic bag. Place on cookie sheet and bake at 350 degrees for 30 minutes.

Hound Dogs

1 8-ounce can tomato sauce
10 hot dogs
¼ cup chopped onions
4 cups mashed potatoes
5 slices American cheese

Slit hot dogs lengthwise and fill each with a teaspoon tomato sauce—
reserve left over sauce. Place in a baking dish. Sprinkle
with onions. Cover with mashed potatoes. Top
with cheese. Bake at 375 degrees for 30 minutes. Pour on rest of sauce and bake 5 more
minutes.

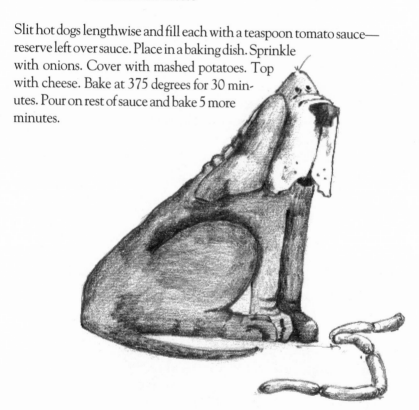

Cowboy Stew

3 tablespoons salad oil
1½ cups sliced onions
10 sliced hot dogs
2 cups stewed tomatoes
3 whole cloves
1 bay leaf
2 cups cooked rice

Saute onions in oil until tender. Stir in remaining ingredients, except rice. Simmer for 15 minutes. Remove cloves and bay leaf. Stir in rice. Pour into greased casserole dish. Bake at 325 degrees for 45 minutes. (You can top with shredded cheddar cheese the last 10 minutes, if you want.)

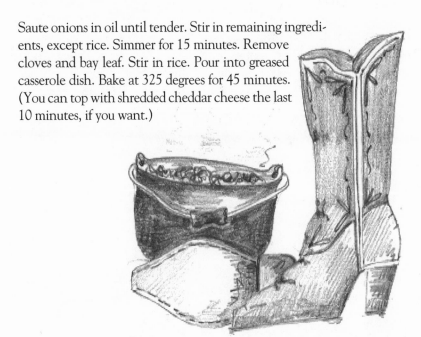

Nutty Noodle

(A '60s favorite at pot lucks)

>2 pounds ground beef
>1 medium chopped onion
>8 ounces small egg noodles
>1 bottle stuffed olives
>1 can cream of mushroom soup
>1 soup can milk
>1 can beef bouillon
>½ pound grated cheddar cheese
>1 cup chow mein noodles
>¼ pound cashews

Brown meat and onion. Cook noodles. Mix meat and noodles with olives, soup, milk and bouillon. Alternate layers of mixture in greased 9x13-inch baking dish with grated cheese. Bake at 350 degrees for 30 minutes. Spread chow mein noodles on top. Sprinkle with cashews. Bake uncovered 30 more minutes.

Potato Pizza

1 pound ground beef
4 cups sliced potatoes
1 sliced medium onion
1 can cheese soup
1 soup can milk
1 15-ounce can tomato sauce
¼ teaspoon salt
⅛ teaspoon pepper
½ teaspoon oregano
¼ teaspoon basil
Dash garlic powder
1 tablespoon butter
6-ounces sliced mozzarella cheese
½ cup grated Parmesan cheese

Brown beef in frying pan. Put potatoes and onion in a greased 9x13-inch baking pan. Spoon beef on top. Stir soup and milk together; pour over beef. Stir tomato sauce and seasonings together. Pour over beef. Dot with butter. Cover with tin foil and bake at 375 degrees for 1 hour. Uncover and place mozzarella cheese on top. Sprinkle with Parmesan

Bread & Breakfast

Beer Muffins

3 cups Bisquick
½ cup sugar
1 12-ounce can beer

Mix all together ingredients until blended. Fill greased muffin tins about ⅔ full. Bake at 400 degrees about 15 minutes or until done. Makes about 2 dozen.

Lemonade Muffins

1¾ cups flour
¼ cup sugar
2½ teaspoons baking powder
¾ teaspoon salt
1 egg
1 6-ounce can frozen lemonade concentrate
¼ cup milk
⅓ cup salad oil
½ cup chopped walnuts
Sugar

Sift dry ingredients. Make a well in center. Beat egg, half of the concentrate, milk and oil. Pour into well and stir quickly, just until moistened. Fold in nuts. Fill greased muffin tins ⅔ full. Bake at 400 degrees for 25 minutes. Turn out on serving dish. Brush tops with remaining concentrate while hot. Sprinkle tops with sugar. Makes 12.

Beer Bread

(In case you can't find the muffin tins)

2 cups self-rising flour
3 tablespoons sugar
1 12-ounce can beer

Follow the same directions as for BEER MUFFINS only pour into a greased loaf pan. Bake at 350 degrees 45-50 minutes or until done. Bread will appear lumpy on top.

Tomato Bread

¼ lukewarm water
1 package yeast
1 teaspoon sugar
2 tablespoons butter
3 tablespoons sugar
2 teaspoons salt
2 cups scalded tomato juice (cooled)
6½ -7 cups flour

Dissolve yeast in lukewarm water with 1 teaspoon sugar, stirring well. In large bowl, beat butter, sugar and salt with tomato juice. Beat in yeast mixture. Stir in flour, a little at a time. When firm dough forms, knead on floured board for 8-10 minutes, until dough is satiny. Place in greased bowl; cover with cloth and let rise in warm (not hot) place for about an hour or until double. Shape into 3 loaves and place in greased loaf pans. Let rise again until double, about 45 minutes. Bake at 350 degrees for 45-50 minutes. Do not let bread get too dark on top.

Mayonnaise Muffins

2 cups self-rising flour
3 tablespoons mayonnaise
1 cup milk
1 teaspoon sugar

Mix all ingredients together. Spoon into greased muffin tins. Bake at 400 degrees for about 15 minutes or until done. Makes 12

Peanut Butter Biscuits

2 cups flour
½ teaspoon salt
2½ teaspoons baking powder
2 tablespoons shortening
¼ cup peanut butter
¾ cup milk

Sift dry ingredients together. Stir in shortening and peanut butter. Slowly add milk to form soft dough. Knead a few times on lightly floured board. Pat to about ½ -inch thickness. Cut into biscuits. Bake on ungreased baking sheet at 450 degrees for 15 minutes. Makes about 16.

Spoon Handle Coffee Cake

1 package dry yeast
½ cup very warm water
⅔ cup evaporated milk
2 tablespoons melted butter
2 tablespoons sugar
1 teaspoon salt
2 cups flour
1 egg
¼ cup evaporated milk
⅓ cup brown sugar
1 teaspoon cinnamon

Stir yeast into water; set aside. In a large bowl, combine ⅔ cup evaporated milk, butter, sugar and salt. Stir in yeast. Beat in 1 cup flour and egg into mixture. Stir in remaining flour. Place dough in greased bowl, turning once. Cover and place in warm spot to rise. When double, divide dough in half and put in 2 8-inch square pans, pressing to fill pan. Cover and let rise until double. With a wooden spoon handle dipped in ¼ cup evaporated milk, make deep holes in dough every 2 inches, leaving 1 inch space around edges. Fill holes with remaining milk. Mix brown sugar and cinnamon; sprinkle over dough. Bake at 375 degrees for 20-25 minutes.

Monkey Ball Cake

(From my neighbor and artist who worked on this book, Kathi Terry)

4 cans refrigerator biscuits (10 to a can)
1 tablespoon cinnamon
¾ cup white sugar
½ cup white sugar
¼ cup brown sugar
1½ sticks butter
Raisins and nuts, if desired

Cut biscuits into quarters. Mix cinnamon and ¾ cup white sugar. Coat biscuit quarters with sugar-cinnamon mixture. Drop into greased bundt or tube pan. Use remaining sugar mixture and add ½ cup white sugar and ¼ cup brown sugar to make 1 cup. Melt butter. Add sugar mixture and bring to a boil over medium heat. Pour over biscuits. Raisins and nuts may be added. Bake at 350 degrees for 45 minutes. Remove from pan immediately. Pull apart. Do not cut.

Ice Cream Muffins

1 cup vanilla ice cream
1 cup self-rising flour

Soften ice cream and mix with flour. Spoon into greased muffin tins, filling ⅔ full. Bake at 425 degrees 12-15 minutes. Makes 6-8.

Gum Drop Bread

3 cups biscuit mix
1¼ cups milk
½ cup sugar
1 egg
1 cup small gum drops (pick out the black ones)
1 cup chopped walnuts

Mix biscuit mix, milk, sugar and egg together. Stir in gum drops and nuts. Pour into greased loaf pan. Bake at 350 degrees for 40-45 minutes.

Eggs in a Hole

1 slice bread
1 egg
Butter
Salt & pepper

Using a glass, cut the center from bread. Melt about 1 tablespoon butter in skillet. Place bread in skillet; break egg into center. Cook over medium heat until egg is set. Turn and cook until done. Add salt and pepper to taste.

Eggnog French Toast

(Something to do with that leftover Christmas eggnog)

    Day-old loaf of French bread
    2 cups eggnog
    Butter
    Cinnamon
    Powdered sugar
    Syrup

Cut bread into 12 ¾-inch slices. Pour eggnog in shallow dish. Place bread in dish and let stand, turning once, until eggnog is absorbed. Melt butter in large skillet or on griddle. Cook slices until golden brown of both sides. Sprinkle with cinnamon and powdered sugar. Serve with syrup.

Cottage Cheese Pancakes

    2 eggs
    ⅛ teaspoon salt
    5 tablespoons flour
    4 cups cottage cheese

Beat eggs well. Stir in salt and flour. Mix in cottage cheese. Cover and let stand 20 minutes. Drop mixture by tablespoon on greased griddle. Fry until brown.

Peanut Butter & Jelly Pancakes

2 cups pancake mix
2 cups milk
2 eggs
½ cup peanut butter
2 tablespoons melted shortening
Butter
Jelly

Combine pancake mix, milk, eggs, peanut butter and shortening in bowl until well-blended but still a little lumpy. Pour about ¼ cup batter for each pancake in greased skillet. Fry on both sides. Spread with butter and jelly. (You can use jam or fruit spread if you want.) Makes about 18-20.

Carrot Bread

2 cups sugar
3 eggs
1 cup salad oil
3 cups flour
¼ teaspoon baking powder
1 teaspoon baking soda
1 teaspoon salt
1 teaspoon cinnamon
2 cups grated, raw carrots
1 cup coarsely chopped pecans
½ cup raisins

Stir sugar, eggs and salad oil together in a large bowl. Sift together flour, baking powder, baking soda, salt and cinnamon; add to mixture in bowl, stirring well. Mix in carrots, nuts and raisins. Pour into two greased bread pans and bake at 350 degrees for about 40 minutes.

Herman

Herman Starter

(Herman became a culinary chain letter in the early 1980's. The idea was to bake two coffee cakes—one for you, one for a friend. Along with the coffee cake, you delivered a jar of Herman starter and recipes. Here's Herman again, along with some recipes my friends included with their Hermanesque creations.)

2 cups flour
1 tablespoon sugar
1 package dry yeast
¼ teaspoon salt
2 cups warm water

In large ceramic or glass bowl, mix flour, sugar, yeast and salt with a wooden spoon. Stir in water; beat until smooth. Cover with towel and set in warm spot overnight. In the morning, feed him Herman food. (After that, you'll need to feed him every fifth day.) Refrigerate, covering loosely with plastic wrap. Stir daily. On the fifth day, feed him again with Herman food. On the tenth day, use 2 cups Herman for cooking, give 1 cup to a friend, and feed the remaining cup with Herman food. Repeat until you run out of friends.

Herman Food

1 cup flour
1 cup milk
½ cup sugar

Herman Coffee Cake

2 cups flour
2 cups Herman
1 cup sugar
2 teaspoons baking powder
1 teaspoon cinnamon
⅔ cup salad oil
2 eggs
½ teaspoon salt
½ teaspoon baking soda
1 cup raisins or mixed dried fruit
½ cup chopped walnuts
Topping

In large bowl, beat together flour, Herman, sugar, baking powder, cinnamon, oil, eggs, salt and baking soda. Stir in raisins and nuts. Pour into two greased 8-inch square baking pans. Sprinkle with topping made by mixing 1 cup brown sugar, 1 tablespoon flour, 1 tablespoon cinnamon, and 4 tablespoons butter. Bake at 350 degrees for 30-35 minutes.

Herman White Bread

1 package dry yeast
1½ cups warm water
1 cup Herman
1½ teaspoons salt
1 tablespoon sugar
About 6 cups flour
½ teaspoon baking soda

In large bowl, dissolve yeast in warm water. Beat in Herman, salt, sugar and 2½ cups of the flour. Cover and let rise in warm spot 1½ hours or until bubbly. Mix 2½ cups flour with baking soda; stir into yeast-Herman mixture. Work in enough flour to make a stiff dough. Turn out on lightly floured bread board and knead 6-7 minutes or until smooth. Divide in half on board; cover with towel and let rest 10 minutes. Shape into 2 round loaves and place on greased baking sheet. Make 3-4 slashes across each loaf with sharp knife. Cover and let rise in warm spot until doubled, about 1 hour. Bake at 400 degrees about 35 minutes or until brown.

Herman Apple Pancakes

2 cups Herman
¼ cup salad oil
2 eggs
2 tablespoons sugar
1 teaspoon salt
1 teaspoon baking soda
1 cup chopped apple (leave peel on)

Mix all ingredients, except apple, in large bowl. Fold in apple. Using scant ¼ cup batter for each pancake, fry on greased griddle until brown on each side—apple bakes as batter is cooked.

Herman Oatmeal Cookies

1 cup brown sugar
6 tablespoons butter
¼ cup shortening
1 cup Herman
1 teaspoon vanilla
1 cup flour
½ teaspoon baking soda
½ teaspoon cinnamon
¼ teaspoon nutmeg
1½ cups rolled oats
1 cup butterscotch chips
½ cup chopped walnuts

Cream sugar, butter and shortening. Mix in Herman and vanilla. Beat in flour, baking soda, cinnamon and nutmeg. Stir in oats, butterscotch chips and walnuts. Drop by teaspoonfuls onto greased cookie sheet. Bake at 375 degrees about 10 minutes. Makes about 48.

Herman Banana Bread

⅓ cup butter
½ cup sugar
1 egg
1 cup Herman
1 cup mashed banana
2 cups flour
1 teaspoon baking powder
½ teaspoon baking soda
¼ teaspoon nutmeg
1 teaspoon salt
1 cup chopped walnuts or pecans

Cream butter and sugar. Beat in egg. Beat in Herman and banana. Sift dry ingredients. Stir into creamed mixture. Add nuts. Pour into greased loaf pan and bake at 350 degrees 1 hour.

Herman Chocolate Cookies

1 cup brown sugar
½ cup shortening
2 eggs
1 teaspoon vanilla
½ cup Herman
1½ cups flour
3 tablespoons cocoa
½ teaspoon baking soda
½ teaspoon baking powder
Chocolate frosting

Cream sugar and shortening. Beat in eggs, vanilla and Herman. Sift dry ingredients and stir into creamed mixture. Drop by teaspoonfuls on greased cookie sheet. Bake at 350 for 8-10 minutes. Cool. Frost with favorite chocolate frosting. Makes about 48.

Cakes

Hot Fudge Pudding Cake

(Fun for the kids—including you—to make. It makes its own gooey fudge sauce right in the baking dish with the cake.)

> 1 cup flour
> 2 teaspoons baking powder
> ¼ teaspoon salt
> ⅔ cup sugar
> 2 tablespoons cocoa
> ½ cup milk
> 1 teaspoon vanilla
> 2 tablespoons melted butter
> 1 cup brown sugar
> ¼ cup cocoa
> 1½ cups boiling water

Mix flour, baking powder, salt, ⅔ cup sugar and 2 tablespoons cocoa together. Add milk, vanilla and butter, stirring until smooth. Spread in a greased 8-inch square baking dish. Mix 1 cup brown sugar and ¼ cup cocoa together. Sprinkle over batter. Pour the boiling water over top. Bake at 325 degrees for 45 minutes.

Keith's Aunt Connie's Dirt Cake

(Everyone will swear this is a flower pot centerpiece)

    4 cups milk
    1 large box instant vanilla pudding
    2 8-ounce packages cream cheese
    1 large carton whipped topping
    20-ounce bag Oreo cookies, crushed

Stir milk into pudding mix and set aside. Soften cream cheese (one minute in microwave) and mix with topping. Stir into pudding mixture—it can be a little lumpy. Alternate layers of crushed Oreos with filling in a large flower pot, ending with Oreos on top. Chill until ready to serve. Insert artificial flowers in straws and poke into mixture, creating a nice-looking arrangement.

Mississippi Mud Cake

1 cup butter
4 eggs
1 cup coconut
2 cups sugar
1½ cups flour
⅓ cup cocoa
⅛ teaspoon salt
2 teaspoon vanilla
1 cup coarsely chopped walnuts
7½-ounce jar marshmallow creme*

In a large bowl, cream butter. Slowly beat in eggs. Stir in coconut, sugar, flour, cocoa, salt, vanilla and walnuts to make a heavy batter. Spread in greased 9x13-inch pan. Bake at 350 degrees for 45-50 minutes. As soon as cake is removed from oven, spread marshmallow creme on top. Let cool for 10 minutes. (Follow directions for icing.)
*6 ounces miniature marshmallows can be substituted

Icing

½ cup butter
6 tablespoons milk
⅓ cup cocoa
1 pound (4 cups) powdered sugar
1 teaspoon vanilla
1 cup coarsely chopped walnuts

Beat all ingredients together, except the walnuts. Stir in ½ cup walnuts (reserve the rest). Spread over cake, swirling through the marshmallow creme. Sprinkle with remaining walnuts.

Indiana Clay Cake

½ cup butter
1 6-ounce package butterscotch chips
1½ cups sugar
½ cup oil
3 eggs
2 teaspoons vanilla
¼ teaspoon red food coloring
1½ cups flour
¼ teaspoon salt
2 cups coarsely chopped walnuts
1 6-ounce package miniature marshmallows

Melt butter and butterscotch chips together. Cool. Cream together sugar, oil and eggs. Mix in vanilla and food coloring. Add flour, salt and 1 cup of walnuts. Mix in the butter and butterscotch. Pour into a greased 9x13-inch baking dish. Sprinkle with remaining cup of walnuts.. Bake at 350 degrees 40-50 minutes. Remove from oven and immediately sprinkle with marshmallows. Cover with tin foil so marshmallows will melt. Spread icing over marshmallows, swirling the two together.

Icing

⅓ cup butter
½ cup brown sugar
2 tablespoons milk
1¼ cup powdered sugar
¼ teaspoon vanilla

Melt butter. Stir in brown sugar and cook over low heat for 2 minutes, stirring all the while. Add milk and bring to a boil, stirring occasionally. Remove from heat and blend in powdered sugar. Add vanilla.

Texas Sheet Cake

2 cups sugar
2 cups flour
½ cup butter
4 tablespoons cocoa
½ cup salad oil
1 cup water
½ cup buttermilk
1 teaspoon baking soda
½ teaspoon salt
2 eggs
1 teaspoon vanilla

Sift sugar and flour into large bowl. In a saucepan, bring butter, cocoa, oil and water to a rapid boil, stirring constantly. Pour over sugar mixture. Stir well; beat in buttermilk, baking soda, salt, eggs and vanilla. Pour into greased 9x13-inch cake pan and bake at 350 degrees for 30 minutes or until done. Immediately spread with icing.

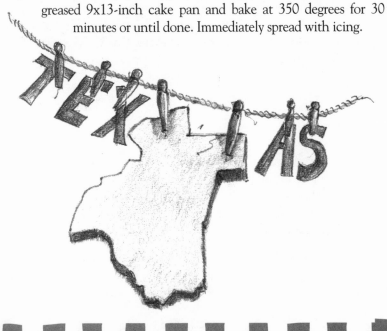

Icing

6 tablespoons butter
4 tablespoons buttermilk
3 tablespoons cocoa
3 cups powdered sugar
⅔ cup chopped walnuts
1 teaspoon vanilla

Heat butter, buttermilk and cocoa to a boil, stirring constantly. Remove from heat and stir in remaining ingredients.

Dark Rum Pudding Cake

1 cup chopped walnuts or pecans
1 large box yellow cake mix
1 small box instant vanilla pudding mix
4 eggs
½ cup cold water
½ cup salad oil
½ cup dark rum

Grease 12-cup bundt pan and sprinkle nuts over bottom. Beat together remaining ingredients until well-blended. Pour over nuts. Bake at 325 degrees for 1 hour. Cool 10 minutes; invert on serving dish. Prick top and sides with fork. Spoon glaze over top and sides, allowing cake to absorb.

Glaze

½ cup butter
¼ cup water
1 cup sugar
½ cup dark rum

Heat all ingredients, except rum, until boiling. Boil 5 minutes, stirring all the while. Remove from heat and stir in rum.

Banana Split Cake

2 cups graham cracker crumbs
1 cup melted butter
2 cups powdered sugar
1 cup butter
1 teaspoon vanilla
1 large can crushed pineapple, well-drained
3 sliced bananas
1 small carton whipped topping
1 cup chopped nuts
1 small jar maraschino cherries, well-drained

Mix graham crackers with butter and pat into 9x13-inch pan. In a large bowl beat powdered sugar, butter and vanilla for 20 minutes. Spread over crumbs. Spoon pineapple on top. Spread whipped topping over pineapple. Arrange a layer of banana slices. Sprinkle with nuts. Place cherries on top. Chill.

Dump Cake

(Can anything be easier? This can be eaten with a spoon standing over the sink.)

> 1 large can undrained crushed pineapple
> 1 can cherry pie filling
> 1 large box yellow cake mix
> 2 sticks butter
> 1 cup coconut
> ½ cup chopped walnuts or pecans

Grease a 9x13-inch baking dish. Pour pineapple in bottom. Spoon cherry pie filling over it. Sprinkle yellow cake mix over top. Put chucks on butter evenly on top. Sprinkle with coconut and nuts. Bake at 325 degrees for about 50-60 minutes.

Lemon Jello Cake

(Remember poking holes in your cakes? Here's one to whip up in less than an hour.)

1 large box yellow cake mix
1 cup water
¾ cup salad oil
1 small box lemon Jello
4 eggs
¼ teaspoon salt
¼ teaspoon lemon extract

Beat all ingredients together for 5 minutes. Bake in a 9-13-inch greased pan at 350 degrees for 35-40. Remove from oven and immediately prick holes all over entire cake with a fork. Spoon topping over cake, smoothing into cake with back of spoon.

Topping

2 cups powdered sugar
6 tablespoons lemon juice

Mix together until well blended.

Zucchini Cake

3 cups sugar
4 eggs
1 cup salad oil
2 teaspoons cinnamon
¼ teaspoon allspice
3 cups flour
1 teaspoon baking soda
1 teaspoon baking powder
½ teaspoon salt
3 cups grated zucchini
1 cup chopped walnuts

Beat sugar, eggs, oil and spices. Sift dry ingredients. Beat into the sugar mixture. Stir in zucchini and walnuts. Pour batter into greased 9x13-inch pan and bake at 350 degrees for 45 minutes. Frost with a cream cheese icing.

No-Bake Applesauce Christmas Cake

(A good kid's recipe—instant results. It looks pretty, too.)

1 small package lime gelatin
1 small package raspberry gelatin
1½ cups applesauce
14 double graham crackers
1 cup whipping cream
¼ teaspoon almond extract
3 tablespoons powdered sugar

Place lime and raspberry gelatin in separate bowls. Add ¾ cup applesauce to each and mix thoroughly. Place two double crackers end to end on serving dish. Spread with ¼ cup lime gelatin mixture. Top with a layer of crackers and repeat with ¼ cup raspberry gelatin. Repeat layers, ending with crackers. Whip cream, adding extract and powdered sugar. Spread over top and side of loaf. Chill one hour. Serves 12-14.

Sauerkraut & Beer Cake

⅔ cup butter
1½ cups sugar
3 eggs
1½ teaspoons vanilla
½ cup cocoa
2¼ cups flour
1 teaspoon baking powder
1 teaspoon baking soda
1 cup beer
⅔ cups rinsed and drained sauerkraut

Cream butter and sugar. Beat in eggs until blended. Mix in vanilla.
Sift dry ingredients together and beat into creamed mixture
alternately with beer. Stir in sauerkraut. Pour into 2 greased 8-inch
cake pans. Bake at 350 degrees for 35 minutes. Frost with favorite
icing.

Gumdrop Fruit Cake

(Well, it sort of tastes like fruitcake. If it doesn't fool anyone, it still is good.)

1-2 pounds large gumdrops (do not use black ones)
1 pound golden raisins
Flour
4 cups flour
1 teaspoon cinnamon
¼ teaspoon cloves
¼ teaspoon nutmeg
¼ teaspoon salt
1 cup butter
2 cups sugar
2 eggs
1½ cups applesauce
1 teaspoon baking soda
1 tablespoon hot water
1 teaspoon vanilla
1 cup walnuts or pecans

Cut gumdrops with scissors into small pieces the size of candied fruit. Mix with raisins; stir in enough flour to coat and mix thoroughly. Sift 4 cups flour, cinnamon, cloves, nutmeg and salt into bowl. Cream butter and sugar in large bowl. Beat in flour mixture alternately with applesauce. Dissolve baking soda in water; add to batter with vanilla. Stir in gumdrops, raisins and nuts. Pour into 2 metal loaf pans lined with waxed paper. Bake at 300-325 degrees for 2 hours. Cool. Wrap in rum or brandy-soaked cheesecloth. Wrap in tin foil. Let stand for at least a week.

Black Bottom Cupcakes

1 8-ounce package cream cheese
⅓ cup sugar
1 egg
⅛ teaspoon salt
1 6-ounce package semisweet chocolate chips
2¼ cups flour
1½ cups sugar
⅓ cup cocoa
1½ teaspoons baking soda
¾ teaspoon salt
1½ cups water
⅓ cup plus 3 tablespoons salad oil
2 teaspoons vanilla

Beat cream cheese, sugar, egg and ⅛ teaspoon salt until smooth. Stir in chocolate chips and set aside. Sift flour, sugar, cocoa, baking soda and ¾ teaspoon salt into large bowl. Beat in water, salad oil and vanilla. Fill paper muffin cups ⅓ full of chocolate batter. Top each with a heaping teaspoon of cream cheese mixture. Bake at 350 degree for 30 minutes. Makes 24.

Pudding Cake

1 large box yellow cake mix
1 small box instant vanilla pudding
¾ cup salad oil
3 eggs
1½ cups 7-Up

Beat cake mix, pudding, salad oil, eggs and 7-Up together. Pour into greased 9x13-inch pan and bake at 350 degrees for about 45 minutes or until done. Cool and frost with icing.

Icing

2 envelopes whipped topping mix
1½ cups cold milk
1 small box instant vanilla pudding mix
½ cup coconut
½ cup chopped walnuts

Beat topping mix and milk until very stiff. Beat in pudding mix. Frost cake. Sprinkle with coconut and walnuts.

Harvey Wallbanger Cake

(Bring out your bell-bottoms for this one)

1 large box orange cake mix
1 small box vanilla instant pudding mix
4 eggs
½ cup salad oil
½ cup orange juice
¼ cup Galliano
¼ cup vodka

Beat all ingredients together for about 10 minutes. Pour into a greased bundt pan and bake at 350 degrees for 45-55 minutes. Cool for 10 minutes. Remove to serving dish and drizzle with glaze.

Glaze

1 cup powdered sugar
1 tablespoon Galliano
1 teaspoon vodka
1 teaspoon orange juice

Beat all ingredients together until smooth.

Fruit Cocktail Cake

(Quick, turn on "I Love Lucy"—the original, not reruns)

2 cups fruit cocktail with juice
2 cups flour
1½ cups white sugar
1½ teaspoons baking soda
¼ teaspoon salt
2 eggs
½ cup brown sugar

Drain fruit cocktail juice into mixing bowl. Beat juice with flour, white sugar, baking soda, salt, and eggs. Stir in fruit. Pour batter into greased 9x13-inch pan. Sprinkle with brown sugar. Bake at 350 degrees for about 35 minutes. Cool. Cover with topping.

Topping

1 cup sugar
1 cup evaporated milk
½ cup butter
1 teaspoon vanilla

Boil sugar, milk and butter for 5 minutes. Remove from heat and stir in vanilla. Pour over cake. Let stand 1 hour before serving. (Ha!)

Tomato Soup Cake

2 cups flour
1 teaspoon baking soda
1 teaspoon baking powder
1 teaspoon cinnamon
¼ teaspoon cloves
¼ teaspoon nutmeg
1 cup sugar
½ cup shortening
1 can tomato soup
2 eggs
1 cup chopped walnuts or pecans
1 cup raisins

Sift dry ingredients together. In a large bowl, cream sugar and shortening, beating until light and fluffy. Add dry ingredients alternately with soup and eggs. (Add 1-2 tablespoons water if batter is too thick). Mix until smooth. Fold in nuts and raisins. Bake in greased bundt pan at 325 degrees for 45 minutes to 1 hour. Cool. Frost with icing.

Icing

1 8-ounce package cream cheese
1 box powdered sugar
½ cup butter
2 tablespoons orange juice
2 teaspoons vanilla

Beat cream cheese, powdered sugar and butter until creamy. Add orange juice and vanilla.

Mexican Wedding Cake

(I don't know if they really eat this is Mexico or not, but we sure ate it in the '70s.)

2 cups sugar
2 eggs
2 cups flour
2 teaspoons baking soda
1 20-ounce can crushed pineapple with juice
½ cup chopped walnuts or pecans

Beat sugar and eggs. Mix in flour and baking soda until smooth. Beat in pineapple and juice. Stir in nuts. Pour into greased 9x13-inch pan and bake at 375 degrees for 35-40 minutes. Frost with cream cheese icing.

Icing

1 pound powdered sugar
1 8-ounce package cream cheese
½ stick butter
½ teaspoon vanilla
4 tablespoons milk

Beat all ingredients together until of spreading consistency.

Scripture Cake

3½ cups flour (I Kings 4:22)
1 tablespoon baking powder (Galatians 5:9)
¼ teaspoon salt (Leviticus 2:13)
1½ teaspoon cinnamon
½ teaspoon nutmeg
½ teaspoon cloves
1 teaspoon ground allspice (I Kings 10:2)
1 cup butter (Judges 5:25)
2 cups firmly packed brown sugar (Jeremiah 6:20)
2 tablespoons honey (Exodus 16:31)
6 eggs (Luke 11:12)
1 8-ounce package dates, chopped (Deuteronomy 34:3)
2 cups raisins (I Samuel 30:12)
1 cup chopped walnuts (Solomon 6:11)
1 cup milk (Judges 5:25)

Sift dry ingredients together; set aside. Beat butter, sugar, honey and eggs until light and fluffy. Mix fruit and nuts together in small bowl; stir in ¼ cup flour mixture. Add remaining flour mixture alternately with milk to butter mixture, beating until smooth. Stir in fruit and nuts. Spoon into greased 10-inch tube pan. Bake at 325 degrees for 1 ½ hours or until top springs back when lightly touched. Cool 20 minutes. Loosen edges and middle with a knife. Turn out on serving plate and cool. Frost or sprinkle with powdered sugar, if desired.

Applesauce Fruit Cake

3 cups sweetened applesauce
1 cup shortening
½ cup sugar
4½ cups flour
4 teaspoons baking soda
1 teaspoon nutmeg
¼ teaspoon cinnamon
1 pound mixed candied fruits
1 pound raisins
¼ pound nuts

Heat applesauce, shortening and sugar, stirring until sugar dissolves. Cool. Beat in flour, baking soda and spices. Mix in remaining ingredients. Bake at 300 degrees about 2-2½ hours in 2 greased loaf pans. Wrap in brandy-soaked cloths for 2 weeks

Watergate Cake

(a.k.a. Pistachio Pudding Cake)

1 large box yellow cake mix
1 cup club soda or ginger ale
1 cup salad oil
1 small box instant pistachio pudding mix
2 eggs
½ cup pistachios or chopped walnuts

Mix all ingredients, except nuts, together in large bowl. Beat for 3 minutes. Stir in nuts. Pour into greased bundt pan. Bake at 350 degrees for 25-30 minutes or until done. Frost with pistachio icing.

Pistachio Icing

1 small box instant pistachio pudding mix
1 cup cold milk
1 small carton whipped topping
¾ cup pistachios or chopped walnuts

Beat pudding with milk until thick and smooth. Fold in whipped topping. Stir in nuts.

Carrot Cake

2 cups flour
1 teaspoon baking soda
2 cups sugar
2 teaspoons cinnamon
½ teaspoon salt
4 eggs
1½ cups salad oil
1 teaspoon vanilla
4 cups grated raw carrots
1 cup walnuts

Sift dry ingredients together into a large bowl. Beat in eggs, oil and vanilla. Stir in carrots and walnuts. Pour into 2 greased 9-inch cake pans and bake at 325 degrees for 40-45 minutes. Frost with cream cheese icing.

Icing

1 8-ounce package cream cheese
¼ cup butter
1 1-pound box powdered sugar
1 teaspoon vanilla
1 cup chopped walnuts
¼ cup coconut

Beat cream cheese, butter, powdered sugar and vanilla together until smooth. Stir in walnuts and coconut.

Better Than Robert Redford Dessert

(Will our kids even know <u>why</u> this recipe was named this in the 1970s?)

1 cup flour
1/2 cup chopped walnuts
1/2 cup melted butter
1 8-ounce package cream cheese
1 cup powered sugar
1 10-ounce carton whipped topping, divided
3 cups cold milk
1 6-ounce box instant chocolate pudding

Mix flour, nuts and butter together; press into 9x13-inch pan. Bake at 350 degrees for 20 minutes. Beat cream cheese, powered sugar and 1 cup whipped topping. Spread over flour mixture. Beat pudding with 3 cups of milk; pour over cream cheese layer. Spread remaining whipped topping on top. Chill and cut into squares.

Coca -Cola Cake

2 cups flour
2 cups sugar
½ teaspoon salt
1 teaspoon baking soda
2 tablespoon cocoa
1 cup butter
1 cup Coca-Cola
½ cup buttermilk
2 eggs
1 teaspoon vanilla
1½ cups miniature marshmallows

Sift flour, sugar, baking soda and salt in large bowl; set aside. Bring cocoa, butter and cola to a boil. Pour over flour mixture. Beat in buttermilk, eggs and vanilla. Stir in marshmallows—they'll float on top of this thin batter. Pour in greased 9x13-inch pan and bake at 350 degrees for about 35 minutes. Cool and frost with cola icing.

Icing

½ cup butter
2 tablespoons cocoa
6 tablespoons Coca-Cola
1 box powdered sugar
1 teaspoon vanilla
½ cup chopped walnuts

Beat together all ingredients, except walnuts. Stir in walnuts.

7-Up Soda Pound Cake

1½ cups butter
3 cups sugar
5 eggs
3 cups flour
3 tablespoons lemon extract
¾ cup 7-Up

Cream together butter and sugar until light and fluffy. Add in eggs, beating well after each addition. Beat in flour, extract and 7-Up. Pour into greased 12-cup bundt pan. Bake at 325 degrees for about 1 hour.

Ice Cream Cake

½ cup butter
55 crushed Ritz crackers
4 small boxes instant coconut pudding
3 cups milk
Half-gallon softened vanilla ice cream
1 small container whipped topping
½ cup coconut

Melt butter in saucepan; stir in cracker crumbs. Press half the crumbs in bottom of 9x13-inch pan; put rest aside for topping. Mix dry pudding, milk and ice cream thoroughly in a large bowl. Pour over cracker mixture in pan. Spread whipped topping over top. Sprinkle coconut on top; sprinkle reserved cracker mixture on top of this. Chill at least 4 hours.

$200 Cake

½ cup shortening
1½ cups sugar
2 eggs
½-ounce bottle red food coloring
3 tablespoons cocoa
1 cup buttermilk
2½ cups cake flour
1 teaspoon salt
2 teaspoons vanilla
1 teaspoon vinegar
1 teaspoon baking soda

Cream shortening and sugar. Add eggs, beating well after each one. Beat in food coloring and cocoa. Add buttermilk alternately with flour. Beat in salt and vanilla. Stir in vinegar and baking soda. Pour into 2 8-inch greased pans. Bake at 350 degrees for about 30-35 minutes. Cool. Frost with icing.

Icing

1 cup cold milk
3 tablespoons flour
½ cup butter
½ cup shortening
1 cup sugar
1 teaspoon vanilla

In a saucepan, stir flour in milk, making a paste. Cook over low heat until thick, stirring constantly. Remove from heat and set aside to cool. Beat butter and shortening until well mixed; beat in sugar. Mix in cooled paste. Stir in vanilla. (You can stir in chopped nuts, if desired.)

Poor Man's Cake

1 cup orange juice
½ cup honey, molasses or corn syrup
½ cup shortening
1 tablespoon cinnamon
1 cup raisins
2 cups flour
2 teaspoons baking powder
½ teaspoon baking soda

In a saucepan, boil orange juice, honey (or substitute), shortening, cinnamon and raisins for 5 minutes. Place saucepan in larger pan filled with ice water. Beat until cool; sift in flour, baking powder and baking soda. Mix well. Pour into greased loaf pan. Bake at 350 degrees for about 45 minutes.

Poorer Man's Cake

1 cup sugar
1 cup raisins
1 cup water
1 stick butter
1 teaspoon cinnamon
1 teaspoon cloves
1 teaspoon salt
1½ cups flour
1 teaspoon baking soda

Boil all ingredients, except flour and baking soda, 3 minutes. Chill. When cool, beat in flour and baking soda. Bake in greased 8-inch pan at 350 degrees for about 30 minutes.

Sauerkraut Chocolate Cake

⅔ cup butter
1½ cups sugar
3 eggs
1½ teaspoons vanilla
½ teaspoon salt
2¼ cups flour
⅓ cup cocoa
1 teaspoon baking powder
1 teaspoon baking soda
1 cup water
⅔ cup rinsed, drained and chopped sauerkraut
½ cup chopped walnuts or pecans

Cream butter and sugar in large bowl. Beat in eggs, vanilla and salt. Sift together dry ingredients. Add dry ingredients alternately with water to creamed mixture. Stir in sauerkraut and nuts. Pour into a greased 9x13-inch baking pan. Bake at 350 degrees for 35-40 minutes. Frost with icing.

Icing

3 tablespoons butter
1 square unsweetened chocolate
1 cup powdered sugar
Warm coffee

Melt butter and chocolate in top of double boiler. Beat in powdered sugar, adding enough coffee to make it spreadable.

Cowboy Cake

1¼ cups flour
1 cup brown sugar
¼ teaspoon salt
½ teaspoon cinnamon
¼ teaspoon nutmeg
⅓ cup shortening
1 teaspoon baking powder
¼ teaspoon baking soda
½ cup buttermilk
1 egg
½ cups chopped walnuts

Mix flour, sugar, salt and spices together. Cut in shortening to make a fine crumb mixture; set aside ¼ cup of the mixture. To remaining crumb mixture, stir in baking powder and baking soda. Mix in buttermilk and egg until just combined. Pour into an 8-inch square greased baking dish. Sprinkle with nuts, then with reserved crumbs. Bake at 375 degrees for 25-30 minutes or until done.

Oatmeal Cake

1 cup quick-cooking uncooked oatmeal
1¼ cup hot water
½ cup butter
1 cup sugar
1 cup firmly packed brown sugar
2 eggs
1 teaspoon vanilla
1⅓ cups flour
1 teaspoon baking soda
¾ teaspoon cinnamon
½ teaspoon nutmeg
½ teaspoon salt

In a small bowl stir oats into hot water and let stand 15 minutes. Cream butter and sugars in medium bowl. Beat in eggs and vanilla. Beat in oatmeal. Sift dry ingredients together and beat into batter. Pour into a greased 9x13-inch baking pan. Bake at 350 degrees for 35-40 minutes. Cool slightly; pour icing over top.

Icing

6 tablespoons butter
½ cup brown sugar
¼ cup evaporated milk
1 cup coconut

Bring all ingredients to a boil in a heavy saucepan; boil 2 minutes. Pour over cake. (You can add 1 cup nuts, if you want.)

Potato Cake

(Heavy and moist)

2 cups sugar
½ cup cocoa
½ cup shortening
1 cup milk
3 eggs
1 cup mashed potatoes
2 cups flour
¼ teaspoon salt
1 teaspoon cinnamon
1 teaspoon cloves
2 teaspoons baking powder
¼ teaspoon baking soda

In a large mixing bowl beat sugar, cocoa and shortening until light and fluffy. Beat in milk and eggs, mixing thoroughly. Beat in potatoes. Sift dry ingredients together and beat well into batter. Pour into greased 10-inch tube pan. Bake at 350 degrees for 1 hour or until it passes the toothpick test. Cool in pan on a rack 10 minutes. Turn out on serving dish. Sprinkle with powdered sugar when cool or drizzle with a thin chocolate icing.

Milky Way Cake

8 regular size Milky Way-type candy bars
½ cup butter
2 cups sugar
¼ cup butter
4 eggs
1 teaspoon vanilla
1¼ cups buttermilk
½ teaspoon baking soda
3 cups flour
1 cup coarsely chopped pecans

Stir candy bars and ½ cup butter in saucepan over low heat until candy melts. Cool. Cream sugar and ¼ cup butter. Add eggs, beating well. Stir in vanilla. Mix buttermilk with soda and add to creamed mixture alternately with flour. Stir in cooled candy bar mixture and nuts. Pour into a greased 10-inch tube pan. Bake at 325 degrees for 1 hour, 20 minutes or until a toothpick inserted comes out clean. Cool in pan 1 hour. Remove to serving plate. Frost with icing.

Icing

2½ cups sugar
1 cup evaporated milk
½ cup butter
1 6-ounce package semi sweet chocolate chips
1 cup marshmallow cream

Stir sugar, milk and butter in saucepan over medium heat until mixture reaches soft-ball stage. Remove from heat. Add chocolate chips and marshmallow cream, stirring until melted. Add milk, if necessary, for spreading consistency.

Wacky Cake

(a.k.a. Crazy Cake or Oil & Vinegar Cake. This was a favorite of mine as a teenager. My mom would throw it together when she saw me dragging home some school friends. The ingredients were always on hand and you made it right in the baking dish. It's wonderfully moist and chewy.)

> 1½ cups flour
> 1 cup sugar
> 3 tablespoons cocoa
> 1 teaspoon baking soda
> ½ teaspoon salt
> ¼ cup plus 2 tablespoons salad oil
> 1 tablespoon vinegar
> 1 teaspoon vanilla
> 1 cup water

Sift flour, sugar, cocoa, baking soda and salt. Pour into an 8-inch square ungreased baking dish. Make three depressions in mixture; pour oil in one, vinegar in another and vanilla in the third. Pour water over all and stir just enough to mix well. Bake at 350 degree for 25-30 minutes. Frost with chocolate icing if desired, but great as is.

Chocolate & Mayonnaise Cake

(An old stand-by)

> 1⅔ cup sugar
> 1 cup mayonnaise
> 1⅓ cup water
> 1 teaspoon vanilla
> 3 eggs
> 2 cups flour
> ⅔ cup cocoa
> 1½ teaspoons baking soda
> ¼ teaspoon baking powder

Mix sugar, mayonnaise, water and vanilla well. Beat in eggs, mixing well. Sift dry ingredients together and gradually beat into mixture. Pour into 2 greased 9-inch pans. Bake at 350 degrees for 30-35 minutes or until done—use the toothpick test to be sure. Cool and frost with favorite vanilla or chocolate icing.

Strawberry Marshmallow Cake

(For a quicker recipe, use a large box of yellow cake mix—preparing as directed—in place of the batter)

1½ cups miniature marshmallows
2¼ cups flour
1 tablespoon baking powder
½ teaspoon salt
1½ cups sugar
½ cup shortening
3 eggs
1 cup milk
1 teaspoon vanilla
1 small box strawberry flavored gelatin
1 16-ounce package frozen strawberries

Sprinkle marshmallows over bottom of greased 9x13-inch baking pan. Sift dry ingredients together; set aside. Cream sugar and shortening until light and fluffy. Beat in eggs, milk and vanilla alternately with dry ingredients. When well-mixed, pour over marshmallows. In a small bowl, mix gelatin granules with strawberries. Spoon over top of cake mixture. Bake at 350 degrees for 40-45 minutes or until done.

Cookies

Potato Chip Cookies I

1¾ sticks butter
2 cups sugar
2 eggs
2 cups flour
2 cups crushed potato chips (crush in plastic bag)
1 teaspoon baking soda
1 12-ounce package butterscotch chips

Cream butter and sugar. Stir into remaining ingredients. Drop by table-spoon onto greased cookie sheet. Bake at 350 degrees 10 minutes. Makes about 5 dozen.

Potato Chip Cookies II

1 cup butter
1 cup white sugar
1 cup packed brown sugar
2 eggs
2 cups flour
1 teaspoon baking soda
1 teaspoon vanilla
1 cup crushed potato chips

Cream butter and sugars. Beat in eggs. Add remaining ingredients, mixing well. Drop by tablespoon on greased cookie sheet. Bake at 350 degrees 10 minutes. Makes about 3 dozen.

Seven-Layer Bars

½ cup butter
1½ cups graham cracker crumbs
1 cup coconut
1 6-ounce package semisweet chocolate chips
1½ cups miniature marshmallows
1 14-ounce can sweetened condensed milk
1 cup chopped walnuts

Melt butter in 9x13-inch pan. Add graham cracker crumbs, patting in place. Layer remaining ingredients in order given. Bake at 350 degrees for 30 minutes. Cool and cut into squares.

Turtle Brownies

1 box German chocolate cake mix
⅔ cup evaporated milk, divided
1 6-ounce package semi-sweet chocolate chips
½ cup coarsely chopped walnuts
1 bag caramels
¾ cup melted butter

Combine dry cake mix with ⅓ cup evaporated milk. Press half of mixture into greased 9x13-inch pan. Bake at 350 degrees for 5 minutes. Unwrap caramels and melt with remaining ⅓ evaporated milk. Sprinkle chocolate chips over partially-baked brownie base. Sprinkle on walnuts. Pour caramel mixture over top. Pat reserved cake mixture into flat pieces with your hands. Lay randomly on top of caramel. Bake at 350 degrees 20-25 minutes.

Monster Cookies

(Wonderful things from the 1970s—you can throw most anything in the way of candy into these)

1 cup butter
1 cup peanut butter
1 cup sugar
1 cup brown sugar
2 eggs
2 cups flour
1 teaspoon baking soda
⅓ cup M & M's
⅓ cup butterscotch chips
⅓ cup semi-sweet chocolate chips

Beat together butter, peanut butter, sugar and brown sugar until light. Add eggs, beating until smooth. Sift flour and baking soda; stir into batter. Stir in M & M's and chips. Drop by ¼ cupfuls onto greased cookie sheets. Flatten slightly with spoon. Bake at 350 degrees for about 10-15 minutes—keep an eye out so they don't burn.

Oven-Broiled S'mores

Graham crackers
Milk chocolate candy bars
Marshmallows

Place graham crackers on cookie sheet and cover each with chocolate square. Top with marshmallow. Broil until golden, about 1 minute. Cover with graham cracker. Eat.

Chocolate Covered Spiders

1 6-ounce package semi-sweet chocolate chips
1 6-ounce package butterscotch chips
1 5-ounce can chow mein noodles
¼ cup chopped walnuts

Melt chips in a saucepan over low heat. Carefully stir in noodles and nuts. Drop by teaspoonfuls onto waxed paper. Let cool. Makes about 3 dozen.

Chocolatines

(What a mess, but oh, sooooo good)

Saltine crackers
1 cup butter
1 cup sugar
1 12-ounce package semi-sweet chocolate chips
1 cup chopped walnuts

Line a jelly roll pan with tin foil. Cover with a layer of Saltines. In a small saucepan, bring butter and sugar to a boil and cook for 3 minutes. Pour over Saltines; bake at 400 degrees for 5 minutes. Remove from oven; cool slightly. Sprinkle chocolate chips on top and spread with back of spoon. Sprinkle nuts on top.

Congo Squares

2¾ cups flour
2½ teaspoons baking powder
½ teaspoon salt
⅔ cup shortening
2¼ cups brown sugar
3 eggs
1 cup chopped walnuts
1 12-ounce package semi-sweet chocolate chips

Sift flour, baking powder and salt. Set aside. Melt shortening and brown sugar. Allow to cool slightly. Beat in eggs, one at a time. Mix in dry ingredients. Stir in nuts and chocolate chips. Pour in greased 9x13-inch pan. Bake at 350 degrees for 25-30 minutes.

 Cookies

This recipe belongs in the category of folk tales, I presume—much like the snake eggs in fur coats and dead cats in shopping bags that show up every decade or so. Depending on your source, the "story" varies in details—like all rumors—but Neiman Marcus always seems to figure into it. Also, like these tales, no one actually knows the real person involved—it's always a "friend of a friend" or "someone my Aunt Bernice knows." This particular version comes from a computer bulletin board. (We're going high-tech with these things now.) It goes like this:

My daughter and I had finished a salad at the Neiman Marcus Cafe in Dallas and decided to have a small desert. Because our family members are such "Cookie Monsters," we decided to try the Neiman Marcus Cookies. They were so good that I asked if they would give me the recipe. The waitress said with a frown, "I'm afraid not." "Well," I said, "would you let me buy the recipe?" With a cute smile, she agreed. I asked how much and she responded "Two fifty." I said with approval, "Just add it to my tab."

Thirty days later I received my statement from Neiman Marcus and it was $285. I looked again and remembered I had only spent $9.95 for two salads and about $20 for a scarf. As I glanced at the bottom of the statement it said "Cookie Recipes—$250." Boy was I upset! I called Neiman's accounting office and told them the waitress said it was "Two fifty" and did not realize she meant $250 for a cookie recipe. I asked them to take back the recipe and reduce my bill, but they said they were sorry, but all recipes were this expensive so not just anyone could duplicate the bakery recipe. The bill would stand. I thought of how I could try to get even or try to get my money back. I just said okay, you folks got my $250 and now I'm going to have $250 worth of fun. I told her that I was going to see to it that every cookie lover will have the $250 recipe from Neiman Marcus for

nothing. She replied, "I wish you wouldn't do this." I said, "I'm sorry, but this is the only way I feel I can get even and I will." So here it is. Please pass it on to someone else or run a few copies. I paid for it, so now you can have it for free. Have fun! This is not a joke—this is a true story!!!!

(That last sentence is debatable.)

    2 cups butter
    2 cups sugar
    2 cups brown sugar
    4 eggs
    2 teaspoons vanilla
    4 cups flour
    5 cups blended oatmeal*
    1 teaspoon salt
    2 teaspoons baking powder
    2 teaspoons baking soda
    24 ounces chocolate chips
    1 8-ounce grated Hershey bar
    3 cups chopped nuts

Cream butter and both sugars. Add eggs and vanilla. Mix together with flour, oatmeal, salt, baking powder and soda. Add chocolate chips, Hershey bar and nuts. Roll into balls and place two inches apart on a cookie sheet. Bake for 10 minutes at 375 degrees. Makes 112 cookies.
*Measure oatmeal and blend in a blender to a fine powder.

Snicker Doodles

(My daughter's favorite to make—and eat—ever since she could reach the kitchen counter, standing on a chair. Fun to say and great eating.)

1 cup shortening
1½ cups sugar
2 eggs
½ teaspoon salt
2 ¾ cups flour
2 teaspoons cream of tartar
1 teaspoon baking soda
½ cup sugar
2 teaspoons cinnamon

Beat shortening and sugar. Add eggs. Beat in dry ingredients, blending well. Roll into balls. Roll balls into small bowl containing mixed cinnamon and sugar. Bake on greased cookie sheets at 400 degrees for 8-10 minutes.

Mouse Ears

1 can refrigerated biscuits
Shortening
1 cup melted butter
½ cup sugar
2 teaspoons cinnamon

Flatten biscuits into thin circles. Fry in hot shortening until light brown. Drain on paper towels. While still hot, brush with butter on both sides and sprinkle with a mixture of sugar and cinnamon.

Elephant Ears

(Must be county fair time)

 1 cup milk
 6 tablespoons shortening
 2 tablespoons sugar
 1 teaspoon salt
 2 packages dry yeast
 4 cups flour
 1 cup sugar
 2 teaspoons cinnamon

Heat milk, shortening, 2 tablespoons sugar and salt over medium heat until scalded (about 5 minutes). Cool to lukewarm. Pour mixture into large bowl; stir in yeast and let stand 5 minutes. Slowly beat in flour. Knead on lightly floured board 5 minutes. Place in greased bowl. Cover let rise in warm spot until doubled, about 1 hour. In the meantime, mix 1 cup sugar with cinnamon. Set aside. Heat 1 inch of oil in skillet until a drop of water sizzles when dropped in. Pinch off 2-inch balls of dough; stretch into 6-inch circle. Fry, 2 at a time, turning once, until golden and puffy. Drain on paper towels and sprinkle while hot with cinnamon-sugar.

An Ode to American Cooking

The ladies shouted, laughed and hugged—
They were a rowdy bunch.
Eating Vinegar Pie, Wacky Cake and Party Dogs,
They declared it one fine lunch.

Next door, the ladies in silence stood
Proper as they could be,
Eating caviar, foie gras and petite fours
While drinking Darjeerling tea.

Where would you rather be?

CME

Forgotten Cookies

(Great for cooks who forget to check on what's in the oven)

> 2-3 egg whites
> ⅔ cup sugar
> Pinch salt
> 1 teaspoon vanilla
> 1 cup semi-sweet chocolate chips

Preheat oven to 350 degrees. Beat egg whites until stiff. Gradually beat in sugar. Mix in salt and vanilla. Fold in chocolate chips. Drop from spoon on ungreased cookie sheets—use up all the batter. Place all cookies in oven and immediately turn off. Leave cookies in closed oven overnight. Makes about 36.

Pies

Soda Cracker Pie

3 egg whites
½ teaspoon cream of tartar
1 cup sugar
1 cup crushed soda crackers
1 teaspoon vanilla
1 cup chopped pecans

Beat egg whites until foamy. Add cream of tartar and beat until stiff. Add sugar gradually. Mix remaining ingredients together and fold into egg whites. Pour into greased pie plate. Bake at 325 degrees for 30 minutes. Chill. Serve with whipped cream.

7-Up Pie Crust

1 cup flour
½ teaspoon salt
¼-⅓ cup shortening
3 tablespoons chilled 7-Up

Sift flour and salt into bowl. Cut in shortening with a fork until mixture is consistency of small peas. Add 7-Up gradually, tossing with a fork to distribute evenly. Press into ball. Let rest 15 minutes. Roll dough on lightly floured surface into ⅛-inch circle. Fit into 9-inch pie plate.

Mile High Ice Cream Pie

(Try your favorite flavor of ice cream; this is just one of many combinations)

        1 9-inch baked and cooled pie crust
        1 pint softened vanilla ice cream
        1 pint softened coffee ice cream
        8 egg whites
        ½ teaspoon vanilla
        ¼ teaspoon cream of tartar
        ½ cup sugar

Spread vanilla ice cream on pie crust. Spread coffee ice cream on top. Freeze until hard, about 2 hours. Beat egg whites with vanilla and cream of tartar until soft peaks form. Gradually add sugar, beating until stiff and glossy. Spread meringue over ice cream to edges of pastry. Broil 30 seconds to 1 minute, until meringue is browned. Drizzle chocolate sauce over each serving.

Chocolate Sauce

1 cup sugar
1 cup half-and-half
2 8-ounce bars German sweet chocolate
2 squares bitter chocolate

In top of double boiler, dissolve sugar in half-and-half. Add chocolates and stir until melted. May be thinned with more half-and-half, if desired. Makes about 1½ cups.

Crazy Crust Apple Pie

(Easy as ...well, pie)

1 cup flour
1 teaspoon baking powder
½ teaspoon salt
1 tablespoon sugar
1 egg
⅔ cup shortening
¼ cup water
1 can apple pie filling
1 tablespoon lemon juice
½ teaspoon cinnamon
Dash nutmeg
2 tablespoons sugar

In a small mixing bowl beat flour, baking powder, salt, sugar, egg, shortening and water in small bowl. Beat well for 2 minutes. Pour batter into a 9-inch pie pan. Mix pie filling, lemon juice and spices. Pour into center of batter. Sprinkle with sugar. Do not stir. Bake at 425 degrees for 45-50 minutes.

Vinegar Pie

¼ cup butter
2 cups sugar
½ teaspoon cinnamon
½ teaspoon allspice
¼ teaspoon cloves
4 eggs, separated
3 tablespoons apple cider vinegar
1 cup raisins
Dash salt

Cream butter and sugar. Beat in spices, egg yolks and vinegar until smooth. Stir in raisins. Beat egg whites with salt until stiff. Fold into filling mixture. Pour into unbaked pie shell and bake at 350 degrees for 15 minutes, then at 300 degrees for 20 minutes or until top is browned and filling is set.

Oatmeal Pie

2 eggs
⅔ cup sugar
½ cup brown sugar
1 tablespoon flour
½ cup dark corn syrup
¼ cup melted butter
1 teaspoon vanilla
⅔ cup quick cooking oats
⅔ cup coconut

Beat eggs and sugars until well mixed. Beat in remaining ingredients. Pour into unbaked 9-inch pie shell. Bake at 350 degrees for 45-50 minutes or until filling is set.

Hershey Bar Pie

3 regular size Hershey almond bars
8 marshmallows
¼ cup milk
½ cup whipping cream
1 teaspoon vanilla
1 graham cracker crust

Melt Hershey bars and marshmallows together. Stir in milk and let cool. Whip cream until stiff; add vanilla. Stir into Hershey bar mixture. Pour into graham cracker pie crust. Chill.

Milky Way Pie

1 package unflavored gelatin
¼ cup cold water
½ cup boiling water
¾ cup milk
6 regular size Milky Way bars
1½ cups whipping cream
⅓ cup powdered sugar
1 teaspoon vanilla
1 baked pie shell

Sprinkle gelatin over cold water in bowl. Let stand 5 minutes. When softened, pour in hot water. Stir until gelatin dissolves. Stir in milk. Melt candy in top of double boiler. Add ½ of gelatin mixture to candy, stirring until smooth. Chill candy mixture and remaining plain gelatin until thick. Whip cream until soft peaks form. Add sugar and vanilla. Stir plain gelatin mixture into whipped cream. Pour alternate layers of candy mixture and whipped cream mixture into pie shell; swirl slightly together. Chill.

Carrot Pie

(A good substitute for pumpkin pie—and no one will know the difference)

2 cups cooked and mashed carrots
½ cup white sugar
½ cup brown sugar
1 teaspoon cinnamon
½ teaspoon ginger
¼ teaspoon nutmeg
⅛ teaspoon cloves
⅛ teaspoon salt
2 beaten eggs
1½ cups evaporated milk

Mix all ingredients together until well blended. Pour into unbaked 9-inch pie shell. Bake at 425 degrees for 15 minutes; turn oven down to 350 degrees and bake 45 minutes longer or until done.

Buttermilk Pie

1 ½ cups sugar
1 cup buttermilk
3 eggs
3 tablespoons flour
¼ cup melted butter
1 teaspoon lemon extract

Beat sugar, buttermilk and eggs together. Mix in flour, butter and flavoring. Pour into 8-inch unbaked pie shell and bake at 325 degrees about 30 minutes or until firm.

Mud Pie

18 chocolate wafer cookies
½ cup soften butter
2 quarts chocolate ice cream
Chocolate syrup
Whipped cream
Chopped walnuts

Crush wafers into crumbs. Mix with butter and pat into pie pan. Chill. Spread partially softened ice cream into shell; mound on top. Freeze 2 hours. To serve, cut into serving sizes, pour syrup on each slice. Top with whipped cream. Sprinkle with nuts.

Impossible Coconut Pie

2 eggs
1 cup sugar
1 cup milk
¼ cup flour
¼ teaspoon baking powder
Pinch of salt
2 tablespoons melted butter
½ teaspoon vanilla
½ cup coconut

Beat eggs, sugar and milk. Sift flour, baking powder and salt together; beat into egg mixture. Stir in butter, vanilla and coconut. Pour into greased 9-inch pie pan and bake at 350 degrees for 30 minutes or until firm.

Peanut Butter Pie

(Guaranteed to push your cholesterol level off the charts)

4 ounces cream cheese
1 cup powdered sugar
⅓ cup peanut butter
1 small carton whipped topping
10-inch graham cracker pie crust
¼ cup chopped peanuts

Beat cream cheese and powdered sugar together. Mix in peanut butter and topping, combining well. Pour into pie crust. Sprinkle with chopped peanuts. Chill until ready to serve.

Mock Apple Pie

(Some people swear there are apples in this. Others say it tastes like lemon pie. Still others will be baffled as to what it tastes like. However, it's guaranteed no one will say it tastes like Ritz crackers.)

    36 Ritz crackers
    2 cups water
    2 cups sugar
    2 teaspoons cream of tartar
    2 tablespoons lemon juice
    1 teaspoon grated lemon rind
    1-2 tablespoons butter
    ½ teaspoon cinnamon

Break crackers into large chunks in bottom of 9-inch unbaked pie crust. In saucepan, heat water, sugar and cream of tartar and boil gently for 15 minutes. Stir in lemon juice and rind. Cool. Pour over crackers. Dot with butter and sprinkle with cinnamon. Adjust top crust and cut slits for steam. Bake at 425 degrees about 30 minutes or until crust is golden.

Candies

Rocky Road

1 12-package semi-sweet chocolate chips
2 tablespoons butter
1 14-ounce can sweetened condensed milk
2 cups walnut pieces
2 cups miniature marshmallows
1 cup halved maraschino cherries (optional)

In top of double boiler, melt chocolate chips and butter. Stir in condensed milk. Remove from heat. Stir in remaining ingredients. Spoon into a 9x13-inch pan lined with tin foil. Chill. Lift foil out of pan, peel off and cut candy into squares.

Million-Dollar Fudge

(Supposedly a Mamie Eisenhower favorite)

  2 cups sugar
  Dash of salt
  1 tablespoon butter
  1 5½-ounce can evaporated milk
  1 6-ounce package semi-sweet chocolate chips
  6 ounces sweet baking chocolate, chopped
  1 8-ounce jar marshmallow cream
  1 cup walnut or pecan pieces

Mix sugar, salt, butter and evaporated milk in a saucepan. Cook over medium-high heat, stirring constantly. When mixture comes to a boil, boil 2 minutes longer, stirring all the while. Remove from heat. Add chocolate chips, chocolate and marshmallow cream. Stir vigorously until chocolate is melted. Stir in the nuts and quickly pour into a greased 8-inch square pan. Cool. Cut into squares.

Mashed Potato Candy

  1 cup cold mashed potatoes
  2 pounds powdered sugar
  1 teaspoon vanilla
  ¾ pound salted peanuts
  1 cup coconut

Mix potatoes, powdered sugar and vanilla thoroughly. Knead in peanuts and coconut. Drop by teaspoons onto waxed paper. Leave until it dries and hardens

Electric Peanut Butter Fudge

2 cups sugar
3 tablespoons butter
1 cup evaporated milk
1 cup miniature marshmallows
1⅓ cups peanut butter
1 teaspoon vanilla

Mix sugar, butter and evaporated milk in an electric frying pan. Set thermostat at 250 degrees and bring mixture to a boil, stirring constantly. Boil 5 minutes. Turn off pan. Stir in marshmallows, peanut butter and vanilla until well blended. Pour into a greased 8-inch square pan. Cool. Cut into squares

Church Windows

1 12-ounce package semi-sweet chocolate chips
¼ cup butter
1 cup chopped walnuts
1 10½-ounce package miniature colored marshmallows
Coconut

Melt chocolate chips and butter in top of double boiler. Cool. Stir in chopped nuts and marshmallows. Sprinkle coconut on waxed paper. Spoon chocolate mixture into four logs; sprinkle with coconut. Rolls and wrap; chill thoroughly. Cut into slices.

Buckeyes

(Another Christmas favorite)

1 pound powdered sugar
1 cup peanut butter
⅔ cup butter
1 teaspoon vanilla
2 ounces semi-sweet chocolate squares
2 teaspoons shortening

Combine first four ingredients in bowl. Chill. Roll into 1-inch balls. Melt chocolate and shortening in top of double boiler. Dip each ball in chocolate, coating only half the ball. Place on cookie sheets covered with waxed paper. Chill. Makes 45-50.

Winter Strawberries

(We make this at Christmas for a treat)

1 large box strawberry gelatin
1 cup coconut
1 cup finely ground walnuts
¾ cup condensed milk
1 teaspoon vanilla
¼ cup sugar
Red food coloring
Slivered almonds
Green food coloring

Mix gelatin, coconut, walnuts, condensed milk and vanilla together in a bowl. Chill 1 hour. Shake sugar with a few drops of red food coloring in small container. Tint almonds with green food coloring. Shape chilled mixture into strawberries and roll in colored sugar. Insert almond sliver to make a stem. Keep chilled in covered container.

Potato Fudge

3 squares unsweetened chocolate
3 tablespoons butter
⅓ cup cooled mashed potatoes
½ teaspoon vanilla
Dash of salt
1 pound powdered sugar

Melt chocolate and butter in top of double boiler. Remove from heat. Mix in potatoes, salt and vanilla. Knead in powered sugar until smooth. Press into greased 8-inch square dish. Cool and cut into squares.

Velveeta-Cheese Fudge

1 pound Velveeta cheese
1 pound butter
4 pounds powered sugar
1 cup cocoa
1 teaspoon vanilla

Melt cheese and butter together in top of double boiler. Remove from heat and stir in sugar, cocoa and vanilla, mixing well. Spread into greased 9x13-inch pan. Cool and cut into squares. (You can add nuts, if you wish.)

Index

Appetizers & Snacks

Beverages

Salads, Vegetables & Jellies

Main Dishes

Breads & Breakfast

Herman

Cakes

Cookies

Pies

Candies

Enjoy the book?

For information on other Eberly Press books, write to:

eberly press

403 Frankfort Ave.
P.O. Box 305
Elberta, MI 49628